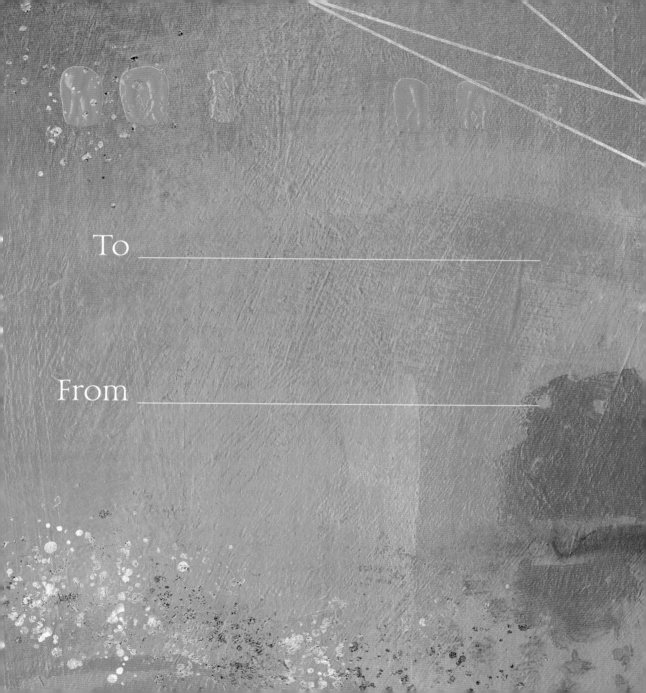

To _____

From _____

Ellie Claire
Hachette Book Group
1290 Avenue of the Americas, New York, NY 10104
ellieclaire.com

First Edition: February 2020

Ellie Claire is a division of Hachette Book Group, Inc. The Ellie Claire name and logo are trademarks of Hachette Book
Group, Inc.

Library of Congress Cataloging-in-Publication Data has been applied for.

Print book interior design by Melissa Reagan.

ISBN: 9781546014522 (hardcover)
Printed in China
RRD
10 9 8 7 6 5 4 3 2 1

she
believes

bonnie rickner jensen
& melissa reagan

Dedication

For my mama, Barbara Jean,
whose constant strength inspired me to believe.

BRJ

My mother believed that there
wasn't anything that I couldn't accomplish.
She gave me wings and the strength to fly.
This book is for you, Shirley Morgan.

MJR

She believes
the best is yet to come.

God is faithful despite our flaws, our falls, and our fickle hearts. He loves us no matter what and He loves to prove it! He wants to move us beyond our doubts to fulfill the desire of our hearts.

She believes
God works miracles in us.

Open this little book to any page, any day, and be reminded of what you believe and Who you believe in. It's going to be good— the gutsy good that comes from hoping long and hanging on.

Do not let your adornment be merely outward...rather let it be the hidden person of the heart, with the incorruptible beauty of a gentle and quiet spirit, which is very precious in the sight of God. 1 PETER 3:3–4 NKJV

She believes

she is an ordinary girl chosen
by an extraordinary God,
and that every day she's
becoming wholly beautiful
in the wholeness of Him.

She believes

she is a light in a world
that's growing dim
to the power of love and the
importance of kindness.
She lives to make a difference
because she has been chosen
by the One who makes
all the difference.

You have been chosen by God himself...you are holy and pure, you are God's very own—all this so that you may show to others how God called you out of the darkness into his wonderful light. 1 PETER 2:9 TLB

She believes
that a giving heart
is a way of life
and the best gifts are free—
a smile, a hug, a tear,
a kind word.

A generous person will prosper; whoever refreshes others will be refreshed. PROVERBS 11:25 NIV

There's more to come: We continue to shout our praise even when we're hemmed in with troubles, because we know how troubles can develop passionate patience in us. ROMANS 5:4 MSG

She believes

that time builds strength,
strength builds patience,
and patience perfects
the purpose
God designed
for her life.

Give yourselves completely to God—every part of you are... to be used for His good purposes. ROMANS 6:13 TLB

She believes
that anything is possible
because everything
is in God's hands.

She believes

she can look to the future
without fear because the One
who created the universe
holds her in the palm
of His hands.

She is clothed with strength and dignity, and she laughs without fear of the future. PROVERBS 31:25 NLT

With the Lord a day is like a thousand years, and a thousand years are like a day. The Lord is not slow in keeping his promise.

2 PETER 3:8–9 NIV

She believes

that time is not in the hands
of a ticking clock but in the hands
of a loving God who sees a bigger
picture and constantly shapes
the minutes and days in her favor.

God is not a secret to be kept. We're going public with this, as public as a city on a hill.... I'm putting you on a light stand. Now that I've put you there on a hilltop, on a light stand—shine! MATTHEW 5:14–16 MSG

She believes
that truth is not something
to be hidden away,
but a foundation
to be built upon.

The LORD directs the steps of the godly. He delights in every detail of their lives. PsALM 37:23 NLT

She believes
God chose this very time
and place to bring her
into the world, and that
He didn't leave her to it,
but every step she takes
belongs to Him.

She believes

that when the storm
is raging all around her
the Prince of Peace
is wrapping His arms
around her making
His peace her own.

Then He arose and rebuked the wind, and said to the sea, "Peace, be still!" And the wind ceased and there was a great calm. MARK 4:39 NKJV

These trials are only to test your faith, to see whether or not it is strong and pure. It is being tested as fire tests gold and purifies it—and your faith is far more precious to God than mere gold. 1 PETER 1:7 TLB

She believes

God alone knows

every part of her heart

and all she has gone through.

He's a loving Father

who not only sees

every pain but transforms

every trial, creating a light

and beauty in her that

is *incomparable*.

She believes

actions have consequences;
and consequences can be a valuable
teacher, a warning to keep her
from straying off the path,
or a light to guide the way.

Joyful are those you discipline, LORD, those you teach with your instructions. PSALM 94:12 NLT

We who have run for our very lives to God have every reason to grab the promised hope with both hands and never let go.

HEBREWS 6:18 MSG

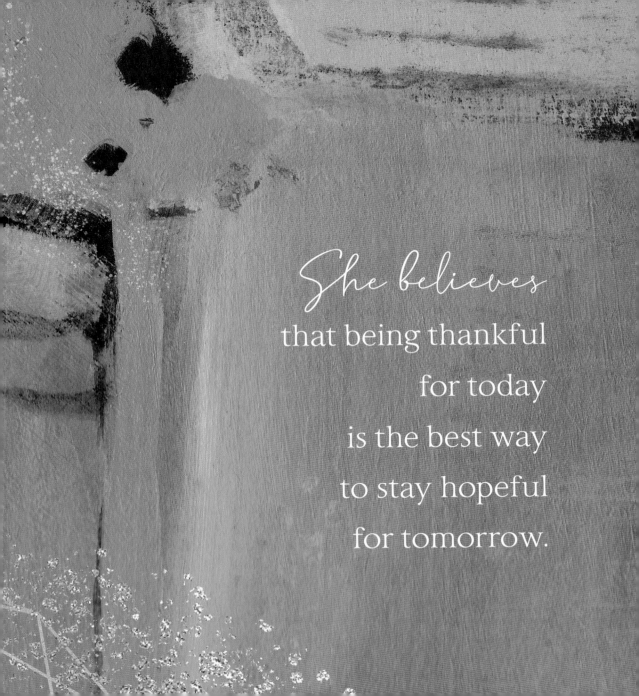

She believes
that being thankful
for today
is the best way
to stay hopeful
for tomorrow.

She believes

the little things that make up
her day are not insignificant.
They are the tiny pieces
of a beautiful mosaic
that is being crafted
by a magnificent Artist.

Thank you for making me so wonderfully complex! Your workmanship is marvelous— how well I know it. PSALM 139:14 NLT

He has showered down upon us the richness of his grace—
for how well he understands us and knows what is best
for us at all times. EPHESIANS 1:8 TLB

She believes

that her journey

will take her to the place

she belongs...

and God's best

will be there

to meet her.

She believes
good things can come
from all circumstances.
Her brave and rescued
soul will never give up
on her true-blue God.

We know that in all things God works for the good of those who love him, who have been called according to his purpose.

ROMANS 8:28 NIV

Anyone who belongs to Christ has become a
new person. The old life is gone; a new life has
begun! 2 CORINTHIANS 5:17 NLT

She believes

that where she came from
does not determine
where she's going,
but that God has a plan
to take her beyond
what she could have
ever imagined
or even hoped for.

She believes

the best way to grow
is to trust that every storm
in life will lift her spirit higher
and her heart closer to God.

You, O LORD, are a shield for me,
My glory and the One who lifts up my head.

PSALM 3:3 NKJV

She believes

that on a day when pulling
the covers over her head is easier
than putting her feet on the floor,
it's a good day to jump up and turn
up the volume of her praise.

You won't see us drooping our heads or dragging our feet!...
It's what we trust in but don't yet see that keeps us going.

2 CORINTHIANS 5:6–7 MSG

Know therefore that the LORD your God is God; he is the faithful God, keeping his covenant of love to a thousand generations of those who love him and keep his commandments. DEUTERONOMY 7:9 NIV

She believes

God can break through
any situation; not because
she prayed a great prayer,
or because she deserves
it in any way, but simply because
she fully trusts that He is
who he says He is.

She believes

that hope stands on courage,
and during the wait
and the heartache

her confidence is ignited
by her fiery spirit
and her faith in the One
who believes in her.

Patience develops strength of character in us and helps us trust God more each time we use it until finally our hope and faith are strong and steady. ROMANS 5:4 TLB

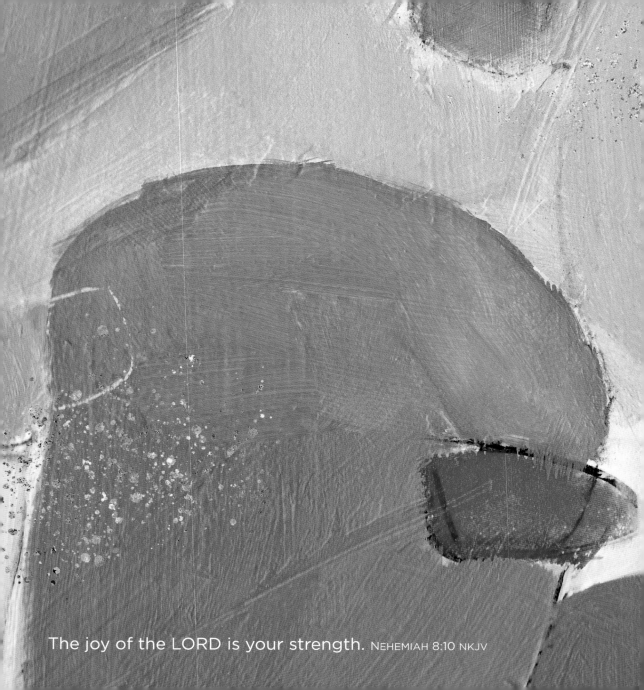

The joy of the LORD is your strength. NEHEMIAH 8:10 NKJV

She believes

joy is her super power.
She chooses it every day
and protects it fiercely
because she believes
that the joy of the Lord
is her strength.
And that strength is invincible.

She believes

it is invaluable to remember
what God has done *for* her,
but even more so what
He has done *in* her—because
that transforms what He can
do *through* her.

Fix your attention on God. You'll be changed from the inside out.

ROMANS 12:2 MSG

He is the faithful God, keeping his covenant of love to a thousand generations of those who love him and keep his commandments.

DEUTERONOMY 7:9 NIV

She believes

that although the future
may seem uncertain,
and tomorrow may look
a bit scary, she will never
have anything to fear
because God is faithful.

She believes

in finding joy
in all the little things God does
for her that no one else sees...
and her heart grows a little
stronger with each one.

He is always thinking about you and watching everything that concerns you. 1 PETER 5:7 TLB

She believes

that her day begins with a clean slate
and a glorious grace—the *all-she-needs*
kind of grace to face whatever
is in front of her.

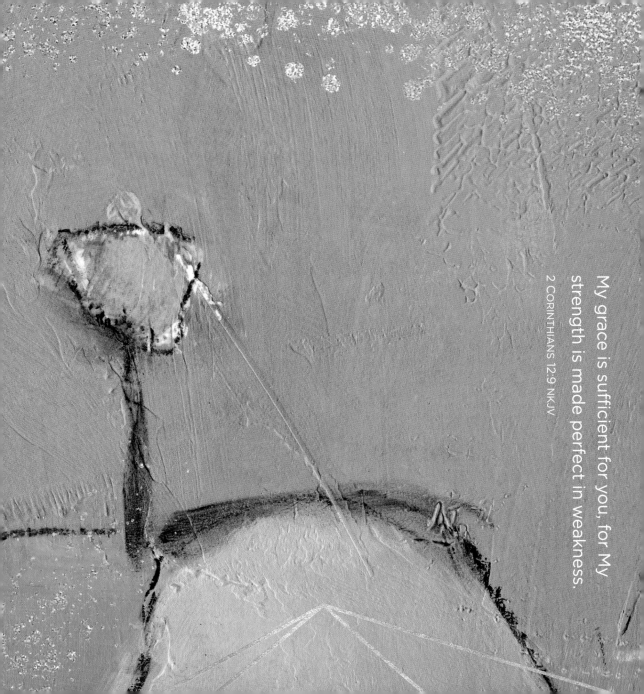

My grace is sufficient for you, for My strength is made perfect in weakness.

2 CORINTHIANS 12:9 NKJV

Instruct the wise, and they will be even wiser. Teach the righteous, and they will learn even more. PROVERBS 9:9 NLT

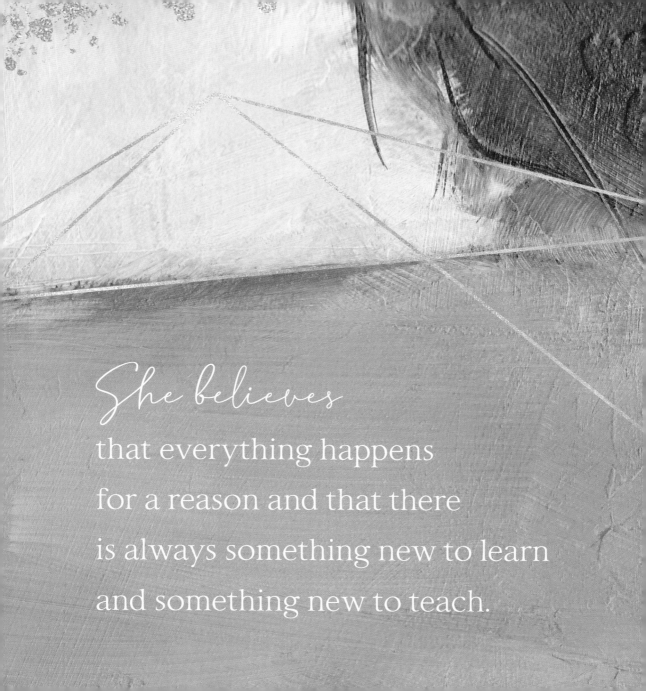

She believes
that everything happens
for a reason and that there
is always something new to learn
and something new to teach.

She believes

God gives her the strength
to keep her head up
and her heart at peace
no matter what the day brings.
Everything that concerns her
concerns Him—and that's all
the confidence she'll ever need.

Be brave. Be strong. Don't give up. PSALM 31:24 MSG

He has sent Me to heal the brokenhearted....
To console those who mourn in Zion, to give
them beauty for ashes....that He may be
glorified. ISAIAH 61:1, 3 NKJV

She believes
in the beauty of grace
and the love that comes
from a heart that's been broken
and put back together
by the gentle hands
of a loving God.

He who began a good work in you will carry it on to completion until the day of Christ Jesus. PHILIPPIANS 1:6 NIV

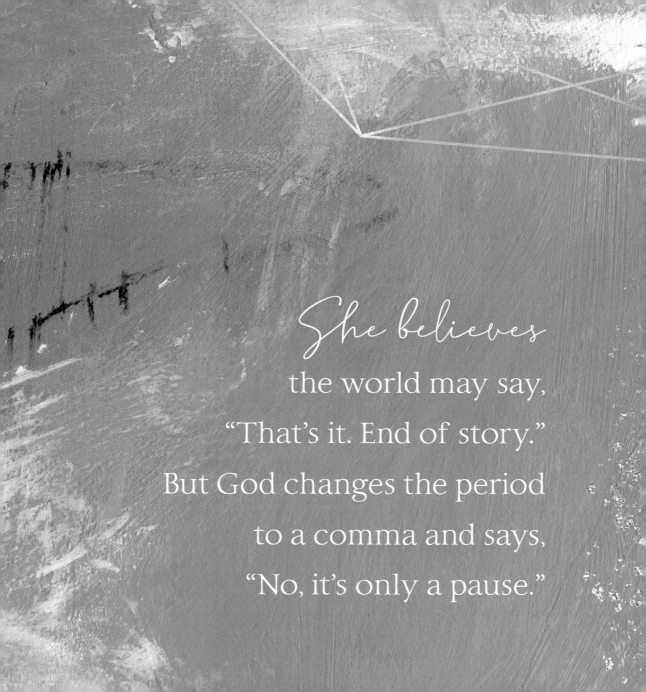

She believes

the world may say,
"That's it. End of story."
But God changes the period
to a comma and says,
"No, it's only a pause."

She believes

climbing the ladder
to her dreams will take
standing tall when she falls short...
looking up when she falls down...
and being still while
God moves mountains.

Glory be to God, who by his mighty power at work within us is able to do far more than we would ever dare to ask or even dream of. EPHESIANS 3:20 TLB

Bless the LORD, O my soul, and forget not all His benefits...
Who redeems your life from destruction, who crowns you
with lovingkindness and tender mercies.

PSALM 103:2, 4 NKJV

She believes

that even when she messes up,

there is a Redeemer

who eagerly says,

"I can fix this."

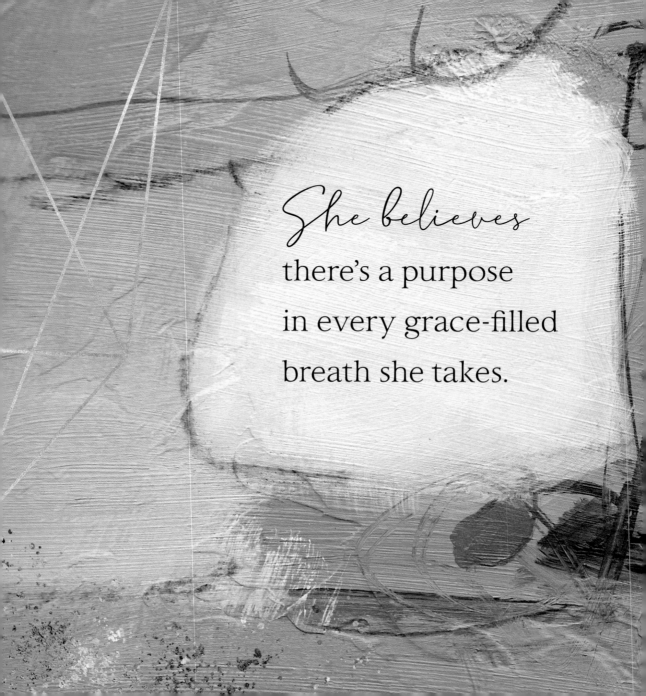

She believes there's a purpose in every grace-filled breath she takes.

It's in Christ that we find out who we are and what we are living for.... He had his eye on us, had designs on us for glorious living, part of the overall purpose he is working out.

EPHESIANS 1:11-12 MSG

She believes

in laughter—jaw-aching,
side-splitting laughter.
The kind where you wake up
sore the next day and know
that you're alive.

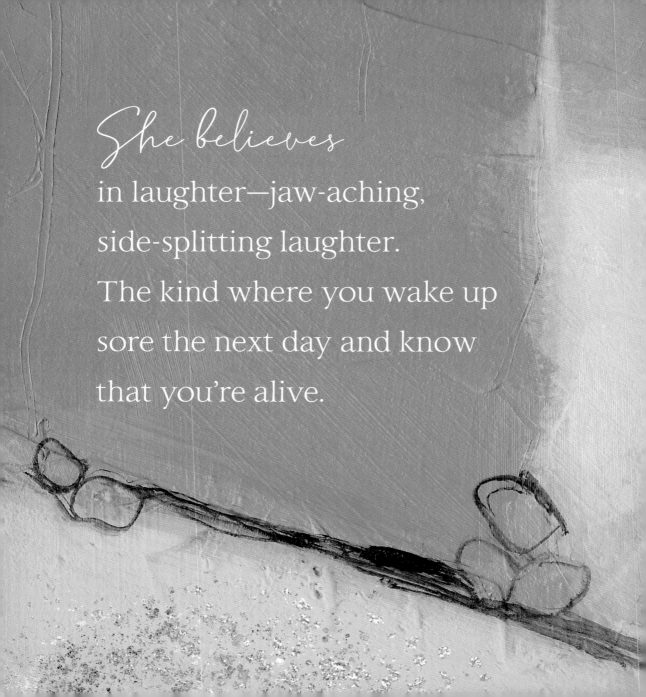

A cheerful heart is good medicine.

PROVERBS 17:22 NLT

But those who hope in the LORD will renew their strength. They will soar on wings like eagles; they will run and not grow weary, they will walk and not be faint.

ISAIAH 40:31 NIV

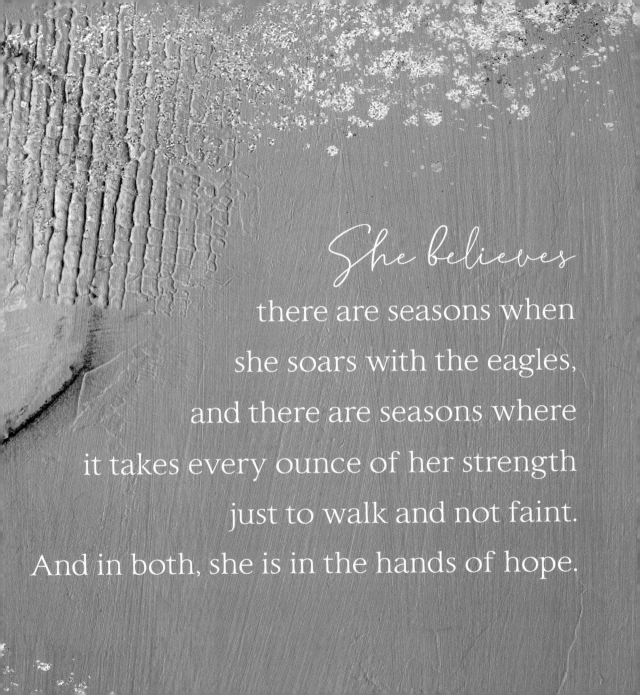

She believes
there are seasons when
she soars with the eagles,
and there are seasons where
it takes every ounce of her strength
just to walk and not faint.
And in both, she is in the hands of hope.

She believes
that kindness can
break down walls.
She has the power
to change the world—
one smile, one word,
one gesture at a time.

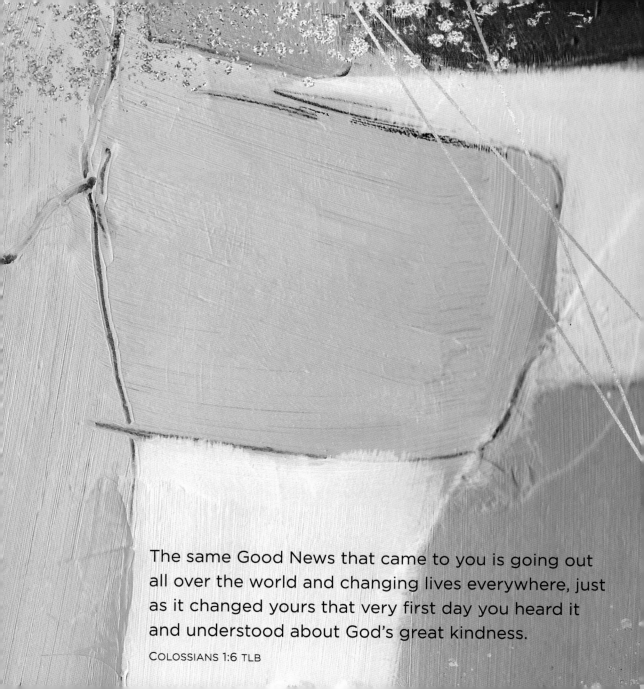

The same Good News that came to you is going out all over the world and changing lives everywhere, just as it changed yours that very first day you heard it and understood about God's great kindness.

COLOSSIANS 1:6 TLB

Through the LORD's mercies we are not consumed,
Because His compassions fail not.
They are new every morning;
Great is Your faithfulness.

LAMENTATIONS 3:22–23 NKJV

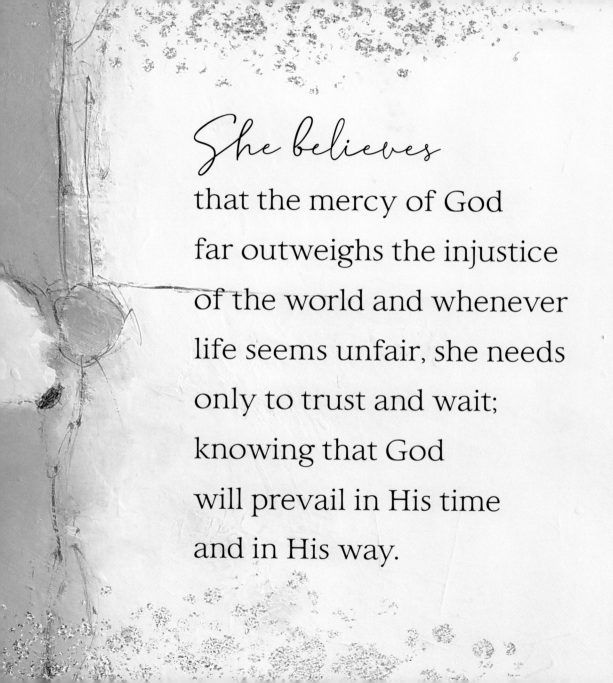

She believes

that the mercy of God
far outweighs the injustice
of the world and whenever
life seems unfair, she needs
only to trust and wait;
knowing that God
will prevail in His time
and in His way.

She believes

grace will hold her in place,
even when circumstances
try to shake her.

Nothing can shake me; he's right by my side. I'm glad from the inside out, ecstatic; I've pitched my tent in the land of hope.

ACTS 2:25–26 MSG

Encourage each other. Live in harmony and peace. Then the God of love and peace will be with you. 2 CORINTHIANS 13:11 NLT

She believes

in looking beyond the flaws
in others to see the hurt
and the struggle and the pain;
and to simply say, "I'm here"
is often more than enough.

She believes

cover-girl perfection is boring
and that beauty is made up
of imperfections, uniqueness,
and kindness of heart.

Charm is deceptive, and beauty is fleeting; but a woman who fears the LORD is to be praised. PROVERBS 31:30 NIV

Be happy, for when the way is rough, your patience has a chance to grow. So let it grow.... For when your patience is finally in full bloom, then you will be ready for anything. JAMES 1:2–4 TLB

She believes

pain is preparation
for the promotion God
has planned—and it's going
to be above and beyond
her wildest dreams.

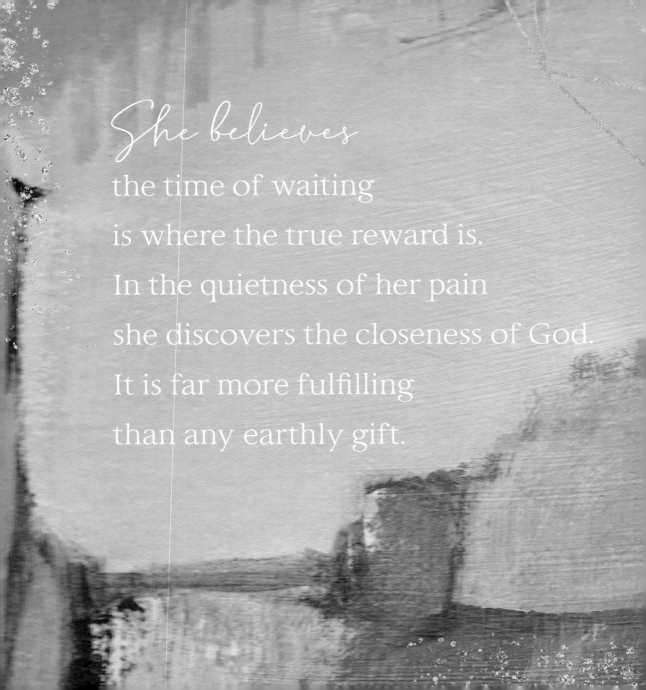

She believes
the time of waiting
is where the true reward is.
In the quietness of her pain
she discovers the closeness of God.
It is far more fulfilling
than any earthly gift.

You will show me the path of life; In Your presence is fullness of joy. PSALM 16:11 NKJV

For I am about to do something new. See, I have already begun!
Do you not see it? I will make a pathway through the wilderness.
I will create rivers in the dry wasteland. ISAIAH 43:19 NLT

She believes

there is a light in her and a light
at the end of her struggle—
she trusts that God knows exactly
where she is in the journey,
and He has amazing and unspeakable
joy planned for her victory.

She believes

that being hopeful
against all odds is the best way
to put all of her trust
in her always-faithful God.

You will do this well, fearless in your struggle, keeping a firm grip on your faith.   1 TIMOTHY 1:18-19 MSG

I have learned the secret of being content in any and every situation, whether well fed or hungry, whether living in plenty or in want.

PHILIPPIANS 4:12 NIV

She believes

life is fragile and strong,

and short and long;

joy and sadness,

goodness and badness;

from beginning to end,

in the trial or the glory

all rolled up into

one exquisite story.

About the authors

BONNIE RICKNER JENSEN is a bestselling author who has written more than thirty children's and gift books. She is the writer behind the bestselling Really Woolly® brand, with more than a million books sold and an ECPA Gold Award-winning *Really Woolly Bedtime Prayers*. She is currently working on a sequel to her recent release *God, I Know You're There* which is available in four languages. Bonnie's inspirations are her three beautiful daughters and six amazing grandchildren. Originally from Napoleon, Ohio, she now writes from her little office in Port Saint Lucie, Florida, where you'll find stacks of picture books, the sound of Mozart, and stashes of dark chocolate.

MELISSA REAGAN is an ECPA Top Shelf Book Cover Award-winning designer type who loves to write almost as much as she loves to design stuff. She most recently contributed to the book *Winds of Heaven, Stuff of Earth* by Andrew Greer, but has also been known to pound out riveting blog entries as well as engaging Facebook posts, though she hardly ever tweets. She is currently living out her dream life in Nashville, Tennessee.